Date:

_____

Dear:

_____

From:

_____

God Cares for You

© 2005 by Roy Lessin

© 2005 Christian Art Gifts, RSA
        Christian Art Gifts Inc., IL, USA

First edition 2005
Second edition 2012

Images used under license from Shutterstock.com

Designed by Christian Art Gifts

Scripture quotations marked AMPLIFIED are taken from *The Amplified Bible*. Old Testament copyright © 1965, 1987 by Zondervan Corporation. New Testament copyright 1985, 1987 by The Lockman Foundation. Used by permission.

Scripture quotations marked KJV are taken from the *Holy Bible*, King James Version. Copyright © 1962 by The Zondervan Corporation. Used by permission.

Scripture quotations marked NKJV are taken from the *Holy Bible*, New King James Version. Copyright © 1979, 1980, 1982 by Thomas Nelson Publishers, Inc. Used by permission. All rights reserved.

Scripture quotations marked LB are taken from the *Living Bible* copyright © 1971. Used by permission of Tyndale House Publishers, Inc., Carol Stream, Illinois 60188. All rights reserved.

Printed in China

ISBN 978-1-77036-751-7

12 13 14 15 16 17 18 19 20 21 – 10 9 8 7 6 5 4 3 2 1

GOD CARES
FOR YOU

ROY LESSIN

✝ christian
art gifts

rk valley of death

afraid, for you close

me, guarding

way. You

r me in

mies. You have

r guest blessings overflow!

goodness and unfailing

Contents

The Lord is my Shepherd

Because the Lord is my Shepherd,
I have everything I need!
He lets me rest in the meadow grass
and leads me beside the quiet streams.
He gives me new strength.
He helps me do what honors Him the most.

Psalm 23

"Even when walking through the

dark valley of death I will not

be afraid, for You are close beside me,

guarding, guiding all the way.

You provide delicious food for me

in the presence of my enemies.

You have welcomed me as Your guest;

blessings overflow! Your goodness

and unfailing kindness shall be

with me all of my life, and afterwards I

will live with You forever in Your home."

Psalm 23:1-6, LB

God's timing

He doesn't always tell you how He will care for you, but He does tell you that you will never be out of His care.

He doesn't tell you when He will answer your prayer, but He does tell you that His timing is always perfect.

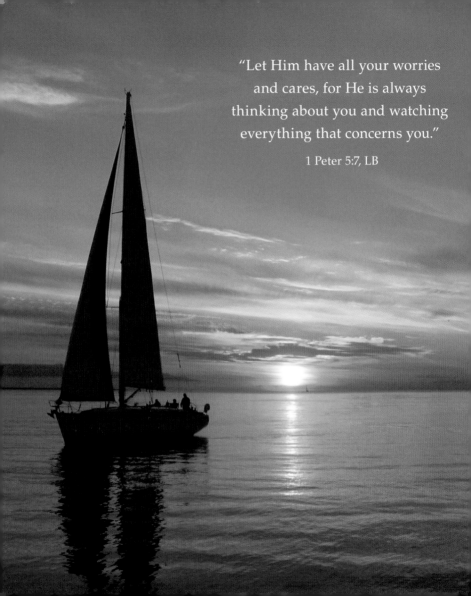

"Let Him have all your worries and cares, for He is always thinking about you and watching everything that concerns you."

1 Peter 5:7, LB

God is wonderful

and does wonderful things.

He is marvelous

and does marvelous things.

What He does

flows out of who He is.

He cannot deny Himself.

He cares for you

God cares for you.

He not only cares about you,

but He takes care of you.

There are many ways

that He reveals His care for you.

One way is through

the names that He bears.

Each name gives us

a deeper insight into His person,

His character and His tender care.

The Almighty God

El-Shaddai means that God is almighty. God is above all things and over all things. He sustains all things, and is the keeper of the life that is committed to Him.

This name also means that God is the One who nourishes and nurtures you as a mother would a child. It is El-Shaddai who does exceeding, abundantly above all that you could ask or think.

He is the sufficient One who will carry out His plans for you to the fullest measure possible.

He provides for you

God is your provider. This is what *Jehovah-Jireh* means. God'
ways of providing for you are far beyond what you are able t
figure out. He has so many ways of meeting your needs that wi
take you by surprise.

When God provides for you it is not only because He sees you
present need, but because He also saw your need in advance. Hi
provision for you has been prepared long before you ever kne
you had a need.

He is your Peace

Jehovah-Shalom means that God is your peace. When people hear the word "peace" they often think of the absence of war, but God's peace means something totally different.

When Jesus was born these words were heard, "Peace on earth ... ". This did not mean that wars had ceased on earth. It meant that Peace on earth was a person. Jesus is the Prince of Peace.

God's peace means that you can have peace with God and the peace of God abiding in you.

God is with you

God is present with you. He is the
God who is there – *Jehovah-Shammah*.
His presence in you is the hope of your life,
the peace in your mind, and the song
in your heart. His presence means
that it is well with your soul.
It is His desire to be at the center
of who you are and all you do.
Where would we be without Him!

Your Healer and your Health

God is your healer and your health. He is *Jehovah-Rapha*.
His healing hands bring sweetness to the bitter waters
of our lives; anointing oil to our wounds;
comfort to our suffering; release to our burdens;
soothing to our tears. God heals, mends,
restores, cures, and renews.

He is your Banner and Victory

Jehovah-Nissi means
that God is your banner.
He is your victory
over every stronghold,
your confidence over every fear,
and your conquering Warrior
over every battle.
He is the flag that you fly high
in your heart, the Captain
that you follow without retreat,
and the name that you shout
in the face of every foe.

He is your Shepherd

God is your Shepherd – *Jehovah-Rohi*. The One who tenderly gently leads you to still waters and green pastures. He goes before you and prepares your way. He is behind you with goodness and tender mercies. It is the name that dries tears and expels fear because His watchful eye is upon you.

"The name of the LORD is a strong tower;
the righteous run to it and are safe."

Proverbs 18:10, NKJV

Wonderful name He bears,
Wonderful crown He wears,
Wonderful blessings
His triumphs afford.
Wonderful Calvary,
Wonderful grace for me,
Wonderful love
of my wonderful Lord.

~ Taken from a chorus

He is the sunrise of your morning,

and the sunset of your day.

His mercy greets you every morning,

and His goodness tucks you in at night.

The Arm of the Lord

The Arm of the Lord is such an awesome name. Through this name God is telling us that His Son is the extension of His might and the expression of His heart. His arm has the power to anoint the eyes of a blind man and restore His sight, and His arm has the tenderness to embrace a little child and draw him to His side.

The arm of the Lord is extended, not to keep you at a distance, but to draw you close to His heart; not to forbid you access to His grace, but to pour it upon you in abundance.

He can carry you because His arms are strong and your needs are great.

He helps you because you cannot help yourself.

He brings you to the place of comfort, hope and healing.

He causes you to regain all that was lost, to renew all that was stolen, and to restore all that was taken away.

The Shepherd and Bishop
of your souls

Stray sheep need someone to find them and bring them back. Sheep cannot figure it out for themselves. Without someone to bring them back into the fold the sheep would remain hopelessly lost.

Jesus is not only the shepherd who finds the lost sheep, but He is also the bishop, or overseer of the sheep. Jesus watches out for the soul of each one that has come to Him for shelter and care.

He has joyfully taken the responsibility to look after you and the spiritual condition of your soul.

"For ye were as sheep going astray;
but are now returned unto the
Shepherd and Bishop of your souls."

1 Peter 2:25, KJV

Hope to your heart

Are you fallen?
Jesus will lift you up.
Are you weary?
Jesus will wipe your brow.
Are you discouraged?
Jesus' touch will restore
hope to your heart.

Are you lonely?

Jesus will draw you close.

Are you afraid?

Jesus will bring you His peace.

Are you confused?

Jesus will guide you back
to His perfect path.

Are you in need?

Jesus will be your supply.

Are you weak?

Jesus will be your strength.

Are you worried?

Jesus will be your source of quiet rest.

"Come to Me and I will give
you rest – all of you who
work so hard beneath a
heavy yoke. Wear My yoke –
for it fits perfectly – and let Me
teach you; for I am gentle
and humble, and you shall
find rest for your souls;
for I give you only light burdens."

Matthew 11:28-30, LB

Wonderful ways
of caring

There are times when God expresses

His care for us through others.

It can be through someone's smile or touch ...

through a timely word that is spoken,

or a loving deed that is expressed ...

through a burden that is shared,

or a prayer that is prayed on your behalf.

In big ways and in little ways God has

so many wonderful ways of caring for you.

God Himself has said, I will not in any way fail you,
nor give you up, nor leave you without support.
I will not in any degree leave you helpless, nor forsake you,
nor let you down, nor relax My hold on you! Assuredly not!
So we take comfort and are encouraged, and confidently
and boldly say; The Lord is my Helper; I will not be
seized with alarm, I will not fear or dread, or be
terrified. What can man do to me?

Hebrews 13:5-6, AMPLIFIED

God wants us to be without any doubts
regarding His care for us.
Having this confidence gives us quiet hearts.
A quiet heart is free from fret and worry.
A quiet heart doesn't have to be in control.
A quiet heart is a confident heart.
A confident heart is a trusting heart.

Our everlasting Peace

"For I am the LORD, I change not."
Malachi 3:6, KJV

everything that God is today, He has always been; everything that He has always been, He will always be. Yesterday, God was there. Today, God is here. Tomorrow, God will be there. Was He your peace yesterday? He will be your peace today. Is He your peace today? He will be your peace tomorrow.

Trust God

There is never a moment in your day
when God says, "You don't have to trust Me now."
   Neither do you ever face a moment
in your day when God says,
"I am not taking care of you now."
   You will never need to
worry about trusting God
too much.

Grace upon grace

When there is a need in your life ...
there is GRACE.
When there is a great need ...
there is GREAT GRACE.
When there is need,
upon need, upon need ...
There is GRACE,
upon GRACE, upon GRACE.

His hand will not let go

When you walk through a dark valley,
no fear shall grip your soul.
When you're climbing a steep mountain,
His hand will not let go.

When you're waiting for an answer
to a prayer in Jesus' name,
It will soon be granted to you –
you won't be brought to shame.

When in a time of suffering
You're seeking for His touch,
His presence will not turn away –
He loves you much too much.

God will not fail you

There's not a promise
He's ever broken,
nothing's failed that He has said.
He will not forsake you,
like the sparrow you'll be fed.
God will not fail you,
He will not leave you alone;
God will not fail you,
He does not forsake His own.

New day –
New needs –
New mercies –
One faithful,
loving, caring God
in the midst of it all!

The Lord your God in your midst, the Mighty One,
will save; He will rejoice over you with gladness,
He will quiet you with His love,
He will rejoice over you with singing.

Zephaniah 3:17, NKJV

Your daily strength

Daily the Lord:

~ bears your burdens (Ps. 68:19).

~ gives you bread (Mt. 6:11).

~ shows you mercy (Lam. 3:22).

~ gives you strength (Is. 33:2).

~ remains faithful (Lam. 3:23).

~ does no wrong (Zeph. 3:5).

~ never fails (Lam. 3:23).

Be not dismayed what-e'er betide,

God will take care of you.

Beneath His wings of love abide,

God will take care of you.

All you may need He will provide,

God will take care of you.

Nothing you ask will be denied,

God will take care of you.

No matter what may be the test,

God will take care of you.

Lean, weary one, upon His breast,

God will take care of you.

~ Civilla D. Martin